Strike It *Happy!*

101 Reflections to Revolutionize Your Life

By Dr. Samantha Madhosingh

Strike It Happy! 101 Reflections to Revolutionize Your Life

Copyright © 2014 Samantha Madhosingh

www.AskDrSamantha.com

ISBN: 978-1503369009

DEDICATION

For my amazingly incredible daughter,

May you always know how deeply you are loved and valued. May you always realize that happiness lives within you and is yours to embrace. And, may you always desire to live a life of love, kindness, compassion, and gratitude.

Get your free eBook to get started!

Magnify Your Brilliance: 5 Keys to a Powerful Life

In this free resource, you will discover how to overcome fear and live a life full of abundance, including how to:

- Discover your purpose and passion
- Dissolve emotional blockage
- Live fearlessly
- Have unshakable self-confidence
- Own your magnificence

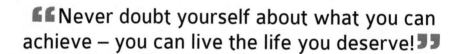

❝Never doubt yourself about what you can achieve – you can live the life you deserve!❞

Dr. Samantha.

Get your free eBook today at www.AskDrSamantha.com

About the Author

Dr. Samantha Madhosingh, known as America's "Holistic Success Doctor®" shows you how to find deep fulfillment and happiness in every single area of your life. Teaching people how to *Strike it Happy™*, she believes that happiness has nothing to do with luck and everything to do with how you view the world, plus your desire and willingness to boldly live out loud. Having spent over 15 years studying the connections between mind, body, and spirit, Dr. Samantha uses practical techniques for change, including advanced cognitive therapy and positive psychology approaches, which will help you change your thinking (and life) forever.

Dr. Samantha received her PsyD. in psychology from The George Washington University and is a clinical psychologist, speaker and sought after expert in emotional wellness, happiness, fulfillment, love, relationships and holistic success.

A frequent media contributor and sought-after expert for both local and national media, she has appeared on FOX, NBC, CBS, Emotional MoJo, Daytime and Heart & Soul. In addition to *Strike It Happy! 101 Reflections to Revolutionize Your Life*, she is the author of *Magnify Your Brilliance: 5 Keys To A Powerful Life*.

Making herself accessible to the public through her newly launched online show "Ask Dr. Samantha," she answers tough questions on love, happiness, fulfillment, self-sabotage, breakthroughs, motivation, living fearlessly, finding your inner power and rekindling the spark in all of your relationships.

Dr. Samantha is a successful businesswoman and devoted mother. She loves exploring the world with her daughter and engaging in the wonderful journey of motherhood. To find about more about her go to

www.AskDrSamantha.com.

What people are saying...

A Brilliant Analogy

Dr. Samantha was the keynote speaker at an event I attended. She spoke powerfully about how those who feel 'stuck' can make the transformational changes necessary to improve their life. She associated getting to the next level in your life with clearing obstacles off an airport runway so the plane can take off. It was a brilliant analogy and everyone in the audience got it! Dr. Samantha is a passionate and very skilled speaker and I highly recommend her to any group.

Jennifer Howard, Professional Coach
Next Level Group

Provided a Blueprint

As a speaker at the Live What You Believe Soul Retreat, Samantha Madhosingh provided a blueprint to experiencing emotional freedom. She shared valuable knowledge and experience that helped the audience understand how to practically apply each key to their own lives. I appreciate the sincere concern from Samantha for her audience and her innate desire and passion to see people healed and free!

Christy Little Jones, MS,
My Relationship Revolution

Remembered Long After

A great presentation is one you remember long after its delivery and Dr. Samantha Madhosingh managed to deliver precisely that at P20 Talks. She exemplified the blend of heart, soul, and wisdom that made our inaugural P20 Talks Conference the success it was. I am still receiving compliments and praise two months post conference and remember her presentation in particular with great appreciation and affection.

Marlaine Cover (Mama Marlaine),
Organizer, P20 Talks Conference,
Author of *Kissing The Mirror*

Introduction

Since the beginning of time, people have been searching for happiness. It's always been this elusive thing believed to be outside of ourselves, like the fancy new car, that important promotion, or the great relationship. Most people spend so much time worrying about other people and what they have or what they think. They start to believe that other people's lives are magical and were sprinkled with some kind of fairy dust but they didn't get any. A lot of people think happiness is something only the lucky get.

In fact, happiness is none of those things. It's really about what's going on inside of you and you being present in your own life. Most of all, it's about the choices you make. Your experiences have gotten you to where you are in your life today. And, every single day you make new choices and can ask yourself this question: "How am I going to live my life today?"

For over 15 years, I have been working with people clinically and they come from all walks of life—from inner city school kids to directors of companies. What I have realized is...

Happiness is a choice.

In our hearts and in our minds we think that we want everything. And we want it all right now. I'm here to tell you that you can have it all, but you can't have it all at the same time. You have to make choices and sacrifices along the way, focus on what's truly important to you. Then, you can achieve happiness in all areas of your life.

What holds us back are the things that we have grown up with that we believe to be true about ourselves. They may come from comments and incidents that occurred that become a part of the dialogue in our heads, leading us to believe we are not good enough or that everything has to be perfect in order for us to be happy. This keeps us stuck in the past and triggers resentment and disbelief in ourselves.

We lack faith in who we are and we believe more in the things that get in our way rather than who we truly are—that's self-sabotage. Once you start that process, you can't be happy.

❝Most people are only successful in about 20% of their lives, but the other 80% is at risk. Maybe you're doing great in your career, but your relationships suffer. Your partner is angry and resentful. Your bedroom has lost that loving connection. Your child won't speak to you. You're stressed beyond belief. Whatever the life issue you are experiencing that feels insurmountable, know that it's not. Your life can change and be extraordinary. You can become successful in 100% of your life.❞

One of the most important things to realize is that your greatest success is just one step beyond your greatest failure.

Life is to be enjoyed. You can reinvent yourself. You can change the way you think. You can make the choices you need to make in order to be happy. Most people only focus their energies on 20 percent of their life—their career and finances. They put all their mental, emotional, and physical energy here, and then they are surprised when they seemingly have everything, but are still unhappy. Instead, the focus should be about holistic success— about being happy in 100 percent of your life. In order to have that, it's important to focus on the things that are truly important beyond career and money. It's also about your physical, emotional, and spiritual health, as well as meaningfully connecting with your family, friends and community. Without these connections, life seems empty.

If you've read hundreds of self-help books or had many hours of therapy, but something still feels like it's missing, read on. I'm here to inspire you in your choices so you can be at peace and have the happiness you deserve.

This book is a tool that can be used to help reset the way you think. I put it together to show you how to reframe negative beliefs and become a more positive person. Use it as the fuel you need to positively energize your thought processes so you can take inspired and powerful action. The result? Greater connections with others and yourself as you lead a more purpose-driven, powerful life and open your heart and mind to all new possibilities.

Table of Contents

Inspired
for Action

1.

❝Happiness is when what you think, what you say and what you do are in harmony.❞

~ Mahatma Gandhi

Happiness begins with the thoughts that you think. You cannot live a positive life with a negative mind because if your mind is negative, everything that follows—the words you speak and the actions you take—will be negative. When your thoughts are positive, and you consciously align them with positive words and actions, you will be unstoppable. It starts inside with what you think and tell yourself.

Action: Notice whether your thoughts and words are reflected in your behavior today. If they are not in alignment, take notice and make an effort to have them match.

2.

❝The view from the top is breathtaking! But it takes patience to get there. Patience is the willingness to keep going, knowing that the way you climb a mountain is by taking one step at a time.❞

~ Dr. Samantha Madhosingh

It's easy to think of a big goal as hopeless because it seems so daunting. That makes you vulnerable to giving up without even really trying. Or you can easily become the world's biggest procrastinator, feeling overwhelmed by the size of the task. When you feel the tension and anxiety building, and the thought of giving up occurs, look for ways you can take just a small step forward.

Action: Break things down into manageable pieces and take it one step at a time and one day at a time. Focus on taking action today and moving forward incrementally.

3.

"Nobody gets to live life backward. Look ahead, that is where your future lies."

~ Ann Landers

For many, life experiences may not always be fondly remembered. The pain that exists from those memories can lead to headaches, stress, and disease. Yet you are the master of your thoughts. When you release the power past life experiences hold over you, the pain will dissipate, and you'll be left with the teaching. Take these pearls of wisdom from their shells and apply the teachings to what lies ahead.

Action: Recognize you are now in the position to live life on your own terms. Be present to what happens today and realize you are in charge now.

4.

❖

❝There's always a light at the end of the tunnel.❞

~ Dr. Samantha Madhosingh

❖

Sometimes in our journey we're faced with difficult times, challenges and chaos. During those times, the situation can seem never ending and hopeless. Know that your darkest place is not a final destination, as things will get better when you keep going, working and growing. Have the faith that as you continue to move forward and take action, the pathway will appear before you. Daylight is on the way, and you will eventually get to where it is you are trying to go.

Action: Stay hopeful and continue to take steps, no matter how small, to keep going.

5.

❝What's holding you back is not what you have, but what you think you're missing.❞

~ Dr. Samantha Madhosingh

Do you ever think like this: "I don't have a college degree, so I'm not qualified." "I don't have the same skill set as that person." "I'm not rich or have money just lying around to spend as she does." This kind of self-talk is nothing other than self-destruction. How can you build yourself or your business up when thoughts such as these bounce into your head? Begin to say, first in your head, and then aloud, sentences that begin with "I am…" I am Strong. I am Beautiful. I am Smart. I am Joyful. I am Peaceful.

Action: Create five positive "I am" statements of your own. Look in your eyes in the mirror and repeat each of them five times.

6.

---❈---

"Whatever is bringing you down, get rid of it. Because you'll find that when you're free... your true self comes out.**"**

~ Tina Turner

---❈---

No pretending, no masks. Before you can be an authentic person in another's eyes, you have to be real with yourself first.

Action: Pick three attributes that you most like about yourself and place all your attention on using these three to move forward.

7.

❝To forgive is to set a prisoner free and to discover that the prisoner was you.❞

~ Lewis B. Smedes

When you are stuck in feelings of anger or bitterness, it's impossible to move forward because the person or situation you are blaming keeps you shackled. Forgiveness is a powerful tool that releases these shackles. When you forgive it doesn't mean you condone the action or person, but instead says you are willing to unburden yourself from the hurt, let yourself heal, and take responsibility for your own life by letting go of the past and moving forward.

Action: Write a letter of forgiveness to a person you feel has hurt you. Be specific in this letter about what you are forgiving. Although you may never send the letter, and this can be a challenging exercise, it helps with healing and letting go.

8.

---❈---

❝Sometimes we have to let go, so we can grow.❞

~Dr. Samantha Madhosingh

---❈---

From the first day of kindergarten to starting that new job, everybody goes through stages in life where what is known is left behind and the unknown is straight ahead. Just like the person on a flying trapeze, one bar must be released in order to grasp the next one.

Letting go of the way things used to be can lead the way to greater personal growth and a more exciting life in the big top.

Action: Think of three ways you may be holding on to something in your past that's no longer serving you. Have your own trapeze release ceremony to let them go and grab hold of the next possibility.

9.

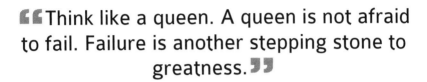

"Think like a queen. A queen is not afraid to fail. Failure is another stepping stone to greatness."

~ Oprah Winfrey

As the leader of your own life, embrace the qualities of being bold, fearless, confident and unapologetic. Step into your own majesty and recognize that the more you live outside your own comfort zone and take chances, the more you will achieve everything your heart desires. You have the power to create in life whatever it is you want.

Action: Even when mistakes are made, the outcome can be new and exciting. Release the idea that failure is bad and realize you are always growing and changing in your own special and unique way.

10.

❖

❝Don't let the noise of others' opinions drown out your own inner voice. And, most important, have the courage to follow your heart and intuition. They somehow already know what you truly want to become. Everything else is secondary.**❞**

~ Steve Jobs

❖

Who do *you* think you are? It's a combination of what you think and what imprint others have made. Sometimes the opinions of others can drown out the messages of your heart and intuition. If you're not living the life you want, it could be because your inner voice needs to be strengthened to better reflect what your heart is saying. That's the voice you want to hear—your true inner self.

Action: To truly know yourself, get very still and allow your intuition to be your guide. When you identify your heart's desire, call on your inner courage to follow that call and step into the life you want.

11.

❝I had to change...because I knew if I wanted my life to be different, I had to be different.❞

~ Dr. Samantha Madhosingh

One of the more difficult things to realize and accept is that your life is a result of your choices. You can move ahead faster if you recognize that it's not about blame or being a victim. If you're not happy with what's going on around you, take a closer look at what's going on within. Consider what you have determined as priorities and what has taken a backseat. Ask yourself if there are ways you can recalibrate your thoughts, feelings and actions to make your life different. How your life unfolds isn't up to anyone but you.

Action: Don't wait for other people to change your life for you. Set goals around who you want to be and how you want to live your life. Take steps to achieve those goals.

12.

❝We are unlimited beings. We have no ceiling. The capabilities and the talents and the gifts and the power that is within every single individual that is on this planet, is unlimited.❞

~ Rev. Dr. Michael Beckwith

You were divinely created to soar. The only limitations on this earth may be what are self-imposed. What's holding you down are thoughts like, "I don't have enough money," "I don't have enough time,, or "I'm too old." If you let your mind fly free, where would it take you? What would you really want to do if money, time, age or expertise weren't weighing you down?

Action: You have a talent and a gift to share. Now is the time to create a strategy around it and move forward, no matter the size of the step.

13.

❀

❝Disappointments are going to happen. Treat them as growth opportunities and learn from them. Flex your bounce-back muscles.❞

~ Dr. Samantha Madhosingh

❀

Stuff happens. Daily detours occur. Inevitably something always comes up to distract us from where we were headed. Perhaps, when your course is changed, you are being re-directed to a better path. Be open to new possibilities and a different journey than you originally envisioned.

Action: When disappointments happen, take a moment to recalibrate your GPS to determine how to get back on track. Then move ahead with confidence to where you are guided in life.

14.

"Spend more time living your values than judging yourself."

~ Dr. Samantha Madhosingh

Many times people say they believe in one thing, yet live something else. For instance, have you noticed how someone will say they value kindness, yet speak critically of others? Or you yourself may say you value confidence, but part of you is hiding in fear. When you truly think about it, your life is a reflection of your values. You can't model what you don't believe.

Action: Evaluate your ideals and how they are being reflected in your life and behavior. Consider what adjustments will bring things more in alignment with your true values.

15.

❝To be a champion you have to believe in yourself when no one else does.❞

~ Sugar Ray Robinson

Champions are born from within. It all starts with knowing what you want and believing in yourself. When you recognize you have that, you don't have to prove anything to others or require their belief in you. Your dreams and goals start with your own belief deep inside. The most important person to believe in you—is you.

Action: Pay attention to the inner voice that knows you have the capability to win and think, "Yes, I can."

16.

❖

❝When you think you're at the end of your rope, tie a knot and hang on.❞

~ Thomas Jefferson

❖

When you think there is nowhere else to go, hang in there. Don't think about giving up or quitting and instead put your attention on the goal. It will give you the strength to persevere even though you think you've run out of energy or options. Sometimes you just have to be patient and wait to see the solution.

Action: Never give up and instead look for ways to go over, under and through. Explore your options and get creative about what answers and solutions are possible. Ask yourself where else you might find solutions.

17.

~ Albert Einstein

How does the fear of making a mistake stop you from trying something new? Mistakes happen all the time and some have incredible, unintended results. Chocolate chip cookies were a mistake made when trying to create a simple chocolate cookie. Silly Putty was to be a rubber substitute made from silicon. Even fireworks were discovered through mistakenly adding together charcoal, sulfur, and saltpeter. Not only do we learn from our mistakes, but some amazing things can happen from them.

Action: Create your own list of activities that you've been tentative about doing because of the fear of making a mistake. Adopt the practice of picking something new from the list to try on a weekly basis.

18.

❝Each of us has our own unique purpose in life and when you know what yours is, you experience greater fulfillment, meaning, and success.**❞**

~ Dr. Samantha Madhosingh

The unfortunate truth is that most people don't follow a path of purpose and passion. They find a job or career that will pay the bills and are always chasing money. It's important to dig a little deeper to identify and understand how you can have fulfillment and joy in your career and in your life.

Action: Explore what you are passionate about and what really excites you. Identify the gifts and talents you possess and share them with your world.

19.

❝Listen to your own voice, your own soul; too many people listen to the noise of the world, instead of themselves.**❞**

~ Leon Brown

There is nothing wrong with listening to what others have to say; it is how you learn, grow, and are shaped as a person. But at the same time you want to develop the strong voice of your inner wisdom. It will become your beacon in a world where it seems every person has something different to say. Learn how to develop and heed your own wisdom inside.

Action: Practice speaking to yourself with a compassionate voice that's free of harsh judgment and criticism. Say loving and kind things to yourself as you would to your best friend.

20.

❝What screws us up most in life is the picture in our head of how it is supposed to be.❞

~ Socrates

Many times we create a belief of how life is supposed to be based on what we observe about others. This comparison can lead to feelings of lack both emotional and physically. There are two things to remember. First, know that you can't shape your life to mirror another's—you were put here to be yourself and live your own purpose. Second, we only see what people show us. You never know what's really going on behind the scenes in their lives. If you did, it might make you appreciate yours much more.

Action: First, take a moment to be grateful for who you are and what you have in your life. Then, identify and embrace your own gifts, talents and abilities and use them to help create the life you desire.

21.

❝Strength comes from within. You are much stronger than you think you are.❞

~ Dr. Samantha Madhosingh

You are strong, and you are resilient. Although life's storms will come, you have the power to withstand more than you think. This strength is grown and sustained by the dialogue you have with yourself. It's important to talk to yourself in a positive, uplifting and loving way to strengthen your inner core so you can be strong, flexible, and bend with the wind.

Action: Grow your inner strength by replacing negative self-talk. Create an inner conversation that uses thoughts and words that are kind, loving and empowering.

23

22.

❝ Just when the caterpillar thought the world was over, it became a butterfly. **❞**

~ Proverb

Unbeknownst to itself, a caterpillar is not in its final state. There are greater plans at work. It has to go through an uncomfortable, maybe even painful, transformation to grow and take flight. But as it unfolds, stretches, and beats its newfound wings it gets stronger and stronger. When it takes off and climbs higher and higher the view is breathtaking.

Action: Accept and embrace change, as it will lead to powerful transformation. Create your "butterfly" goal with specific steps that will lead you to grow, develop, and fly high.

23.

“You alone are enough; you have nothing to prove to anybody.”

~ Maya Angelou

One of the biggest obstacles to our joy and happiness is the feeling we're not "good enough" to be loved or to be successful. The truth is that whoever you are, wherever you come from, you are deserving of these things and more. You don't have to earn it—it's yours from the start.

Action: Sit with someone you trust and ask them to describe your positive qualities. Look them in the eyes, listen carefully, and absorb what they have to say.

24.

❝Emotionally strong people are able to bounce back from life's challenges and find ways to grow from difficult situations.**❞**

~ Dr. Samantha Madhosingh

Life is filled with times of joy and times of challenge. It's the challenging times that make your life a richer experience as it gives you a chance to grow and learn more about yourself. You may not immediately come to know the reason behind the curve or obstacle, but you have the power to stand back up, dust yourself off, and keep on going—stronger for what you have faced and overcome.

Action: When less than ideal situations occur, take a deep breath and ask yourself, "What can I learn from this experience?" Keep that learning in mind as you move forward to new challenges and successes.

25.

❝If we did the things we are capable of, we would astound ourselves.❞

~ Thomas Edison

People are incredibly capable; yet many times they stop themselves from shining brilliantly. What if you were designed to be the person to discover the next life-saving vaccine? Or your words would inspire greatness in another? You have the ability to do amazing things. Stop holding yourself back and instead allow yourself to experience life at full capacity. Show the world you are something special.

Action: Identify ways you are holding yourself back and then list five ways you can break through those barriers and let your light shine.

26.

———————————— ❖ ————————————

❝You know all those things say you've always wanted to do? Go do them.❞

~ Dr. Samantha Madhosingh

———————————— ❖ ————————————

Most people create a "bucket list," yet never think about what steps to take to cross items off. What are you waiting for? What's really stopping you? The longer you wait to act on your dreams, the more you put life on hold—and it doesn't wait around until you're ready. Live today because tomorrow is not promised. Go and have fun.

Action: Pick three things you've always wanted to do, but have been putting off for some reason, and go do them.

27.

❝Do not judge me by my successes, judge me by how many times I fell down and got back up again.❞

~ Nelson Mandela

When you ask someone about how they succeeded, you'll most likely hear stories of failure and times when things didn't work and hope was almost lost. But then there's a spark—a reason that things turned around and victory became theirs. When you have a mission and a passion, do not quit, even in the face of mistakes and challenges. Recognize they are part of life and that they, too, will become part of your story of success.

Action: Do not quit, making mistakes is part of life. Move forward. Failure and making mistakes are part of the journey to success.

28.

❝Catastrophic thinking serves no purpose other than to make us scared and miserable.❞

~ Dr. Samantha Madhosingh

Stop expecting the next disaster. Instead, think about what could go right. Retrain your mind to expect success. What might your life be like if you achieved your dreams? The millisecond a doubt or fear-filled thought begins to form, immediately transform it into a positive one, envisioning the life will have when you achieve this dream.

Action: Fill in the sentence: "My steps for success today are…"

29.

❝To get ahead in life you have to take chances. Don't live life fearful of what comes next. That's not what living is about.❞

~ Dr. Samantha Madhosingh

Living life each day can be challenging enough without having to worry about what might happen if you fail at going for your dream or goal. But without taking a risk, any risk, to achieve that success, you are in danger of not living a purposeful life.

Action: Determine and take even the smallest step you can take that will allow you to move toward your goal.

30.

❝Courage doesn't mean you don't get afraid.
Courage means you don't let fear stop you.❞

~ Bethany Hamilton

Everyone feels afraid at times. The question is, do you have the resources to draw on to see you through fear and not let it stop you? You do if you have courage. Make it a priority to cultivate an inner feeling of courage to be your companion as you go forward.

Action: When you feel fear, ask yourself, "What is the real danger here? And is that a valid reason not to do it?"

31.

❝Peace. It does not mean to be in a place where there is no noise or hard work. It means to be in the midst of all those things and still have calm in your heart and mind.❞

~ Unknown

The brain doesn't function at its best unless it's calm. But this can be hard to remember when you're in the middle of a stressful situation and the body goes into "fight or flight" mode. If you cultivate a feeling of inner peace, you'll lessen the extent of stress on your body and mind. When you're able to think clearly, you'll find situations you used to think were chaotic are just another part of the day.

Action: A key technique to for developing inner peace is to practice deep breathing for at least 15 minutes a day. Be sure to inhale, hold and exhale your breath for a count of five each. This will teach your body and brain how to relax so you can stay calm in stressful situations.

32.

—❈—

❝Courage doesn't always roar. Sometimes courage is the quiet voice at the end of the day saying, 'I will try again tomorrow.'❞

~ Mary Anne Radmacher

—❈—

Being courageous isn't always about being loud and bold. It can instead center on the act of moving forward, even when you don't seem closer to your goal. It's about persevering and continuing on faith knowing that tomorrow is a new day.

Action: At the end of the day, consciously exhale all the stresses and disappointments of the day and inhale all the hopes and possibilities of tomorrow.

33.

❝Truth be told, nothing in life is to be feared, it is only to be understood.❞

~ Marie Curie

When you feel afraid, pause and take another look. Most times the fear you feel stems from anxiety of the unknown. This anxiety can distort things and make them seem bigger and "badder" than they really are. Instead, challenge the fear and reframe your thoughts on it. This will help it shrink and allow you to continue on your journey of self-discovery.

Action: Identify how fear shows up in your life and ask yourself how might you be distorting reality. Once you are able to see there is no real danger, take action and challenge the fear so you can have a life of freedom and clarity.

34.

"You can have many great ideas in your head, but what makes the difference is the action. Without action upon an idea, there will be no manifestation, no results, and no reward."

~ Miguel Ruiz

You are full of brilliant ideas. Yet there's a big difference in having an idea and moving forward to making it a reality. Taking too long to think about a strategy without taking action may prevent you from writing the next bestselling book or creating a revolutionary household gadget. The good news is that it all starts with making a decision. Follow that with a step of activity and you are on your way!

Action: Consider your best ideas and create a strategic plan listing the actions that will bring those ideas into reality. Now take the first critical steps to implement your actions and look for the positive results!

35.

❝Don't be scared of failing. Instead be scared of a life of regret that comes with not trying.❞

~ Dr. Samantha Madhosingh

Ask people who are happy with their lives and they will tell you—they failed much more often than they succeeded. The key is not to have regrets later about what you didn't do and instead live your life now. Take stock of the things you say you want to do—and start doing them! Create a life you can look back on and be happy about because you didn't let fear stand in the way.

Action: Take a leap of faith and do something you've been holding back on. Live a life of no regrets, starting today.

36.

"Your past is just a set of experiences you give meaning to. It does not define you. The only power it has is the power you give it.**"**

~ Dr. Samantha Madhosingh

Many people relive and rehearse past experiences again and again until it becomes part of their present. It's one thing to learn from your past, it's another to let it hold you hostage. By carrying this burden, today's choices and experiences can be stifled. Instead, take the lessons the past has to offer and then release its power over you.

Action: Identify what stories from the past you are bringing into the present. Look to see how you can reframe your perspective on your story to take the lesson, give it a more positive meaning and move on.

37.

---·❀·---

**"If your compassion does not include yourself,
it is incomplete."**

~ Siddhartha Gautama

---·❀·---

People often spend a lot of time being judgmental of others. Most times what they say about other people are really feelings and criticisms they have about themselves. There are others who are sweet and complimentary to others and then awful to themselves. Look for ways to nurture feelings of compassion, kindness, and love - not only for others, but yourself, too.

Action step: Practice noticing when you beat yourself up inside your mind with words. Stop doing it. Instead, treat yourself with compassion, kindness, and love. Be your own best friend.

38.

❝I keep my mind focused on peace, harmony, health, love and abundance. Then I can't be distracted by doubt, anxiety or fear.❞

~ Edith Armstrong

Difficult life experiences can lead to toxic beliefs that clog our minds with negativity. Your brain has created neuropathways that keep these beliefs alive and circulating over and over again. Transformation comes from forming new pathways in your mind, retraining it with positive thoughts, and engaging with positive people. The more you focus on using empowering words and thoughts, the more you can open yourself up to growth.

Action: Pay attention to the words you are using. Are they positive or negative? If you start your sentences with "I can't" or "I don't" chances are what follows is negative. Armed with this knowledge, practice using empowering or more positive dialogue both internally and externally— what you say to yourself and to others.

39.

❝The enjoyment of life is all about the journey. If you stay focused only on the end goal, you will miss out on all the fun!❞

~ Dr. Samantha Madhosingh

In life, it's all about the journey—the process of getting to where you're going. When you are solely focused on the end goal, you miss the magical points along the way. Instead, consider the relationships, connections, fun and excitement, and even the trials and tribulations, you experience. Be present in the life you have right now, and enjoy it all!

Action: Look for ways to live in the moment, connect with people around you, and have fun in your day. Before retiring for the day, ask yourself: What was the best thing that happened today?

40.

❝Beauty is about being comfortable in your own skin. It's about knowing and accepting who you are.**❞**

~ Ellen DeGeneres

Being comfortable in your own skin no matter where you are on your journey of personal growth and development is a sign of self-love. Many times people think that because they are growing or changing it is okay to hate the place where they are now. That's the worst thing you could do because it keeps you stuck. Instead, love the person you are now—the person who is growing and changing every step of the way. Learn to appreciate both your flaws and your strengths for they make you who you are.

Action: Embrace your perfectly imperfect self—the whole you. Remind yourself that you are perfect, whole, and complete just the way you are.

41.

"Faith is taking the first step even when you don't see the whole staircase."

~ Martin Luther King, Jr.

Although we would all love to have a crystal ball, living a full life means being able to take steps even though you don't know what's going to happen next. It comes from having faith in yourself and the belief that things will work out. If nothing else, you will gain wisdom in what steps to avoid in the future. You don't always know what the outcome will be but that's no reason to stay paralyzed and not climb the staircase of life.

Action: Take your first steps in faith toward an unmet goal.

Notes

Strike It Happy!

44

Notes

Notes

Strike It Happy!

_____

_____

_____

_____

_____

_____

_____

_____

_____

_____

Notes

Affirming Your Power

42.

❝Being self-confident means not letting other people shape or shake who you are.❞

~ Dr. Samantha Madhosingh

Self-confidence is a strong belief in your own abilities and has a significant impact on your actions and behaviors. It is important to not keep looking for the approval of others to validate who you are or who you want to be. Instead, hold yourself in positive regard, accept yourself fully, and embrace your entire being.

Today's mantra: I am enough!

43.

"Happiness is not a possession to be prized, it is a quality of thought, a state of mind."

~ Daphne DuMaurier

Happiness is a choice. No matter who you are, where you have been or what you have been through, in this very moment you have a choice whether you want to live the day in peace or in chaos. You have a choice in your attitude and whether or not you will call yourself "happy."

Today's mantra: I choose happiness.

44.

❝The history of the world is full of men who rose to leadership, by sheer force of self-confidence, bravery and tenacity.❞

~ Mahatma Gandhi

A new idea or dream has come to mind. But you're afraid that it may not come to fruition. Believe in yourself and your dream so you can muster up the courage to plant the seed and stand your ground. Boldly and unapologetically design the life you desire.

Today's mantra: I am brave.

45.

❖

❝Other people's opinion of you does not have to become your reality.❞

~ Les Brown

❖

At your core, there is a strong soul that cannot be shaken or swayed by experience or opinion. It stays true to you, no matter what. You want to get to know this inner self and rely on its strength when ego is tempted to doubt your worthiness. Don't allow others' opinions or your own doubts to creep in casting shadows on your soul and the truth it knows for you.

Today's mantra: I know I am worthy.

46.

---※---

❝Opposition is a natural part of life. Just as we develop our physical muscles through overcoming opposition – such as lifting weights – we develop our character muscles by overcoming challenges and adversity.**❞**

~ Stephen R. Covey

---※---

There are no true barriers to stop you. The only thing that can halt your progress is being unwilling to find a way over, through, or around obstacles that appear. When you come upon one, pause and think about the best way to move forward. Live a life of confidence and adopt a "never quit" attitude. Be bold!

Today's mantra: I am unstoppable.

47.

—◆—

❝Do the best you can until you know better. Then when you know better, do better.❞

~ Maya Angelou

—◆—

We all go through life thinking we are doing the best we can, but are we really? It's a healthy practice to look for ways to make incremental improvements in your words, choices, and actions— the small things that keep you out of a "thinking rut." You'll see that when you begin to look for ways to harness the power you have in your thinking and doing, things get better and better every day.

Today's mantra: I have the power to change my life.

48.

❀

"Be nice to yourself... It's hard to be happy when you are being mean to yourself all the time."

~ Dr. Samantha Madhosingh

❀

Unfortunately, people are generally mean to themselves. It's difficult to be happy when you've created the story that you're unlovable, unworthy, or undeserving and must always feel guilty when you focus on yourself. It creates an inner turmoil that doesn't allow happiness in and keeps you stuck. Instead, challenge the mean things you think and treat yourself with compassion. Practicing self-care isn't selfish, it is a gift you deserve. Stop the tirade of "I should haves" and instead accept that you are good enough and always have been.

Today's mantra: I accept myself as I am.

49.

❝Accept what is, let go of what was, have faith in what will be.❞

~ Sonia Ricotti

One of the great miracles of being human is the ability to have perspective on the past, live in the present, and dream of the future. This perspective is a gift and one that shouldn't be taken lightly. Your very presence, your uniqueness, your life journey are all very special. You are a living, walking example of the magic that exists on this planet. Embrace everything you are and all that you have to offer.

Today's mantra: I am a miracle.

50.

❝Put yourself in a state of mind where you say to yourself, 'Here is an opportunity for me to celebrate like never before, my own power, my own ability to get myself to do whatever is necessary.'**❞**

~ Anthony Robbins

You are one powerful human being. You have the strength and wherewithal to achieve any and every single dream you want to accomplish. That fortitude is found within you.

Today's mantra: I am capable of doing whatever I set my mind to do.

51.

" Stay close to anything that makes you glad you are alive. "

~ Hafez

Sometimes, our mind plays tricks on us. We only see what we perceive as being wrong with the world and ourselves. The result is not being open and aware of the good that is all around us. Instead, be conscious of how you think and who you surround yourself with. One of the first steps in realizing your dreams is being open to receive them.

Today's mantra: I am open to receive the miracles of this day.

52.

❝Your life is too valuable to live without passion and purpose!❞

~ Dr. Samantha Madhosingh

Have you ever stopped to think about the miracle of life? Of being born, growing up, and seeing the abundance of the planet through your very own eyes? What an incredible gift! There's also the gift inside each of us—the brilliance you were given to share your magnificent self with the world. You are an amazing being who also serves as a beacon of light for others. Breakthrough any fears and turn up that dimmer switch, your purpose is waiting.

Today's mantra: I am designed to shine my beautiful light brilliantly.

53.

"The future belongs to those who believe in the beauty of their dreams."

~ Eleanor Roosevelt

Occasionally the challenges or mistakes of the day can eclipse the vividness of your dreams and goals. Sometimes, instead of brushing it off, we repeat the story of what went wrong over and over to ourselves and others. Instead of rehearsing and reliving the negative, use your imagination to bring your dreams to life. Think of what you want in life every day—and visualize the life you are ready to live.

Today's mantra: I am ready to live my dreams.

54.

❝Keep your thoughts positive because your thoughts are the fuel of your actions.❞

~ Dr. Samantha Madhosingh

The inner chatter you hear is stopping you from doing what you want to do. The words are cutting and biting deep into your soul. "Who are you to change the world? Why do you think you can succeed at this massive goal?" Simply respond, "Why not me?"

Today's mantra: I let go of all the mental clutter that is distracting me from my greatness.

55.

**❝You, yourself, as much as anybody in
the entire universe, deserve your love and
affection.❞**

~ Buddha

Many times we can be nice to others, but nasty to ourselves. The
compassion we may show others is lost when it comes to giving
ourselves a break. This can grow until we become conditioned to
the negative self-talk and don't even notice it any more. And
when that happens, we become our own worst enemy. When you
remind yourself to show more love to the world, make sure you
share some of that good feeling with yourself.

Today's mantra: I love myself unconditionally.

56.

❝The thing that is really hard, and really amazing, is giving up on being perfect and beginning the work of becoming yourself.❞

~ Anna Quindlen

Letting go of the concept of being perfect is both a little step and a big step. It can be hard to loosen your grip on the notion that everything must be "just so." But it's a sign of growth to let go and let be. Once you do, a whole new world can open up before you—one that's rich with being "as is." This is applicable to the things around you—and you yourself. Notice the beauty of being okay with what is around you and in you.

Today's mantra: Even though I am not perfect, I choose to love myself anyway.

57.

" Intuition is always right in at least two important ways; it is always in response to something, and it always has your best interest at heart. "

~ Gavin de Becker

It's said that creating a plan is the best way to success. But what comes before the plan? Many leaders will tell you it is intuition— listening to an inner voice. In the morning, before the hustle and bustle of the day starts, surrender to the peace and silence, and pay attention to what's asking to be heard. Allow you inner self to guide your day.

Today's mantra: I will allow my intuition to guide me.

58.

---

⁶⁶Fear is strong, but faith is stronger yet.⁹⁹

~ Norman Vincent Peale

Fear often arrives early in life, almost like an infection, until it becomes a part of us and leads to a constant feeling of apprehension and anxiety. To release fear and anxiety, tap into your faith, hope, and courage. Welcome them into your thinking and allow them to take residence in you. Take a moment to breathe in belief and joy, and exhale worry and concern.

Today's mantra: I let go of my fears and worries.

59.

"You could make a wish or you could make it happen."

~ Unknown

You may have heard the saying "hope is not a strategy." The same is true for wishes that are not backed by the belief that they can come true. You're not given a dream without also being given the means to make it happen. It all starts with the feeling that it can become reality for you. Believe with all your heart, take action, and watch your dreams come true.

Today's mantra: Yes I can! Yes, I can! Yes, I can!

60.

❝How does one become a butterfly?" she asked pensively. "You must want to fly so much that you are willing to give up being a caterpillar.❞

~ Trina Paulus

You have already had many growth opportunities in your lifetime. Being born was the first! You pushed your way through to escape the tiny space, which could no longer hold you. Perhaps you did the same by continuing on with your education. That's the way life works—we grow and stretch and make room until the new space starts to feel small. And then we grow and stretch again.

Today's mantra: I am like a butterfly, pushing through and spreading my wings.

61.

"The will to win, the desire to succeed, the urge to reach your full potential...There are the keys that will unlock the door to personal excellence."

~ Confucius

Each person who graces this earthly plane has something special to give. It starts with the feeling inside of the potential you have to offer and your willingness to share it with the world. As you do, your belief in your own gifts and your confidence will grow, along with your satisfaction that you left your mark on the world.

Today's mantra: I recognize my gifts and believe in myself.

62.

❝Keep your face always toward the sunshine, and the shadows will fall behind you.❞

~ Walt Whitman

Your experiences growing up have shaped who you are today. But, if you continue to relive those times, especially the tough, challenging ones, you will not be able to move forward and create the life you want now. You cannot change what's happened in the past, but each new day is a clean slate upon which you can create a new pathway to your future.

Today's mantra: I let go of my past so I can create the future I desire.

63.

"It isn't where you come from; it's where you're going that counts."

~ Ella Fitzgerald

You have overcome a lot in your life. Believe it. Have faith that you are now in charge of the outcome of your life, and are capable of achieving your dreams, desires, and destiny. You have built the inner muscle necessary to go forth and light the way for others.

Today's mantra: I am strong and I am ready to shine.

64.

---------------------◆◆◆---------------------

❝Don't let what you can't do stop you from doing what you can do.❞

~ John Wooden

---------------------◆◆◆---------------------

Yes, you've had some challenges in your life. But you've also been given strengths. Those strengths wouldn't develop without having the push of challenges to overcome—that's what creates your ability to tap into your own power. When challenges arise, use them as an opportunity to grow and notice how strong you really are.

Today's mantra: I believe in my ability to live a powerful life.

65.

❝Honoring your uniqueness is the greatest gift you can give yourself.❞

~ Dr. Samantha Madhosingh

Have you ever known someone who is oblivious to how important they are or what they have to offer humanity? Sometimes you can get so involved or preoccupied in your own inner world that you don't notice the light you're casting on others. You were specially designed in your own unique way to share your brilliance. Appreciate who you are and embrace your gifts.

Today's mantra: I choose to see the light that I am in this world.

66.

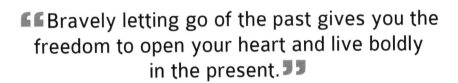

❝Bravely letting go of the past gives you the
freedom to open your heart and live boldly
in the present.**❞**

~ Dr. Samantha Madhosingh

Clinging to the past blinds you to your present. Instead, give yourself permission to let go of what's been and instead live in the here and now. Absorb the idea that there are new possibilities and opportunities that exist right now and you have the ability to recognize and savor them.

Today's mantra: I cannot change the past so I will live in this present moment.

67.

❝It is easy to dodge our responsibilities, but we cannot dodge the consequences of dodging our responsibilities.❞

~ Josiah Charles Stamp

You have the power. You have the tools. You get to choose how you will take the actions necessary to create what you desire in your life. Notice your role and responsibility to yourself and the world around you. You can tap into experts and specialists to help you, but it is you alone who is at the helm of your ship.

Today's mantra: I am completely responsible for my present and my future.

68.

**❝The difference between try and triumph is just
a little 'umph!'❞**

~ Marvin Philips

There are days that seem never ending with their challenges. It seems constant: the dings of incoming email, the beeps of texts, and the disruption of people needing attention. Yet it can only get to you if you let it. Regaining focus and energy can be as easy as closing your eyes, taking a breath, and getting centered with a clear mind. Make a conscious decision to triumph over distractions and make your day productive. Then, give yourself a power hour, turn off those electronics, and tackle that to-do list.

Today's mantra: I will be focused and productive in everything I do today.

69.

❝I've missed more than 9000 shots in my career. I've lost almost 300 games. 26 times, I've been trusted to take the game winning shot and missed. I've failed over and over and over again in my life. And that is why I succeed.**❞**

~ Michael Jordan

What if you thought of mistakes not as burdens, but as fuel for future success? And the more fuel you put in the tank, the faster you would reach your success? That's exactly how it works. The more you do, the more you succeed. Reframe the way you think of mistakes and instead use them to fire you up for success.

Today's mantra: I will learn from my mistakes not be burdened by them.

70.

---◆---

"The less you react to negative people, the more peaceful your life will become."

~Dr. Samantha Madhosingh

---◆---

It's going to happen—negative people will exist in your life. It may feel like they are responsible for making you feel angry or sad, but know that you have a choice. You can choose to let them affect you or not, and decide how you will respond. In addition, you can grow further by trying on a different perspective to see things from their point of view. When you do this, life will become more peaceful, and you'll radiate that peace towards others.

Today's mantra: I will replace my anger with understanding and compassion.

71.

---◆◆◆---

❝Life is a balance of holding on and letting go.❞

~ Rumi

---◆◆◆---

What if you danced with the challenges in life instead of fighting them? It's easier to gently release that which doesn't serve you and hold on to that which does. Remember, too, that the challenges and successes that surround you on the dance floor of life don't define you. You have the ability to find solutions. No matter what comes in life, you can choose to handle events with grace and strength.

Today's mantra: My struggles don't define me. I can find solutions.

Notes

Notes

Notes

Notes

Living
in Gratitude

72.

"Nothing can dim the light which shines from within."

~ Maya Angelou

It's time to embrace one important fact. You are lovable, important, and worthy. Whether you believe it or not, you are uniquely designed to share a beautiful light that exists within you. Even though you may have challenges and frustrations in your life, you can immediately change the way you feel by one simple action—smiling. It lifts your spirit and connects you with others.

Gratitude in Action: Smile more. Consciously spend the day smiling...to yourself and to those you meet.

73.

❝How people treat other people is a direct reflection of how they feel about themselves.❞

~ Paul Coelho

People are put in front of us for a reason—to love, even if it's only through a glance or a smile. All people want to know that they matter. When acknowledgment occurs between two people, a certain kind of magic happens not only for the receiver, but for the giver too. It makes a soul happy to connect with another and be recognized.

Gratitude in Action: Acknowledge every person who crosses your path. Look up at them, take a moment to look them in the eye, smile, and say "Hello."

74.

---- ❧ ----

❝Use gratitude to help you put things in perspective.❞

~ Dr. Samantha Madhosingh

---- ❧ ----

During busy days, it's common to lose perspective and be impatient, wanting others to move faster and do more. But think how much more enjoyable the journey would be if you took a breath, slowed down, and put into practice more patience. One way to ground yourself and calm down is to bring gratitude into your day. Turn things around by noticing how you can be thankful for all the opportunities you have and the presence of others in your life.

Gratitude in Action: Have more patience for someone with whom you are often impatient, such as your kids, family, employees, neighbors, or colleagues.

75.

❝I love myself for I am a beloved child of the universe and the universe lovingly takes care of me now.❞

~ Louise Hay

No matter who you are, you are an amazing miracle–divinely created. When you think you have made a mistake, remember this: Nobody's perfect, we're all simply human. Make an effort to be more kind and gentle with yourself in thoughts, words, and actions. Remember, you are the only *you* that there is. Take care of yourself.

Gratitude in Action: Look yourself in the eye in your mirror and say, "I love you!" Take a deep breath. Repeat it at least 10 times. Say it out loud and really listen to your voice.

76.

❝There is more hunger for love and appreciation in this world than for bread.❞

~ Mother Teresa of Calcutta

People live on more than food. To live well, they crave something that only other humans can provide: love and appreciation. Even though friends and family may know how much you care about them, they may feel they are being taken for granted. Letting someone know how much you value their love, loyalty, and friendship can brighten anyone's day—including your own.

Gratitude in Action: Tell three people in your life how much you appreciate them. And then, tell them why.

77.

❝Forgiveness is the greatest gift you can give yourself. It's not for the other person.❞

~ Maya Angelou

Someone has hurt you. Forgiving them, does not mean you accept what they did or approve of it. It just means that you will no longer allow them, the negative energy, or the issue that you're angry about have power over you any longer.

Gratitude in Action: Think of someone you are still holding a grudge with or are angry with. Close your eyes, take a few slow deep breaths, and then make a committed decision to forgive them, accept them as who they are, and let it go.

78.

❝The true measure of a man is how he treats someone who can do him absolutely no good.❞

~ Samuel Johnson

Throughout the day you are presented with a myriad of opportunities to engage with others. You can look at each of these chances to see what's in it for you, or you can look at each one as an opening to practice kindness, compassion, and paying it forward.

Gratitude in Action: Help someone with absolutely no expectation that they will do anything for you in return.

79.

❝The secret of change is to focus all of your energy, not on fighting the old, but on building the new.❞

~ Socrates

Pay very close attention to your thoughts. Are they positive or negative? Do you judge or criticize a lot? How often are you critical of yourself? Recognize that the voices you hear within can sometimes be harsh and look for ways to soften them. Create new words and images for the exciting new possibilities you are creating for your life.

Gratitude in Action: Write down the positive things you could say to yourself when "You're not..." is heard. Now, practice saying, "I am beautiful." "I am smart." "I am enough."

80.

❝Kind words are a creative force, a power that concurs in the building up of all that is good, and energy that showers blessings upon the world.❞

~ Lawrence G. Lovasik

You are meant to build people up, not tear them down. When your actions are thoughtful, considerate, compassionate, loving, and kind, each person you connect with experiences you in this manner. Leave your mark on this world by engaging them in positive interactions. It will be part of your legacy.

Gratitude in Action: Spend today only with positive words at the focus of your thoughts and your conversations.

81.

**❝Words only hurt when you choose
to believe them.❞**

~ Dr. Samantha Madhosingh

Angry words have been directed to you from another and it hurts. Yet, it's your choice whether or not to own the hurt along with the words. When you commit to engage in a resolution that does not come from a place of emotion, things become more clear and easier to talk about. Take the emotional charge out of the words and have a thoughtful conversation instead.

Gratitude in Action: Have a talk, sans emotion, with the person you need to clear the air with.

82.

❝Let us be grateful to the people who make us happy; they are the charming gardeners who make our souls blossom.❞

~ Marcel Proust

Many people in this world go about their day in service to others. There are the more familiar jobs—those who wait on you in restaurants and deliver your newspaper. Then there are those who quietly serve, such as the driver who busses your children from school to home, or the men who climb the electric poles to keep the electricity humming. There are also those in the military doing their duty day in and day out. Everyone deserves to be remembered for the contributions they offer.

Gratitude in Action: Find a way to thank and support someone for his or her service.

83.

"Take the time to do what makes your soul happy."

~ Dr. Samantha Madhosingh

When you go after a dream it may seem to run away from you, getting further and further from being achieved. The trick is to stop chasing it and create a strategy for the dream to come true. This strategy comes with creating a specific vision of what you want. Consider what you want to be doing and how you want to feel during the day. Define what it is you are reaching for so you recognize it when you achieve it.

Gratitude in Action: Write down the vision you have for your life. Then write down three things you will commit to doing to bring you closer to that vision.

84.

❝Three things in human life are important: the first is to be kind; the second is to be kind; and the third is to be kind.❞

~ Henry James

Showing kindness can be as simple as a note of appreciation and gratitude to someone who helps you in some way. Tell your loved ones how much you appreciate them, how amazing they are, and how much you love them. You can even extend this kindness to the store clerk, the friend who checks in on your beloved pet, the neighbor who had a cup of sugar when you needed one. Plus, you can practice being kind to yourself by looking in the mirror and saying how much you love and appreciate you!

Gratitude in Action: No matter where in the world you happen to be, practice kindness today.

85.

❝I've been helped by acts of kindness from strangers. That's why we're here, after all, to help others.❞

~ Carol Burnett

The movie *Pay It Forward* was a surprise hit. The concept of expressing an act of kindness you received by extending an act of kindheartedness to another gained world-wide attention. For many, it has become a regular part of their daily life, with people performing random acts of kindness for others every day. Helping others helps us stay anchored in happiness.

Gratitude in Action: Give assistance to someone who hasn't asked for it, but are in need. It could be someone you know, someone you know only a little, or even someone you don't know at all.

86.

❝I would maintain that thanks are the highest form of thought, and that gratitude is happiness doubled by wonder.❞

~ Gilbert Keith Chesterton

The person who holds the door or elevator open…the waiter/waitress at the restaurant…the person who lets you in during traffic…the supermarket cashier…your child care provider. The act does not have to be large in size for you to be grateful in receiving it. Also, what you received may not always be pleasant, yet it brought a new awareness. Giving thanks for every event, yes, even the rough ones, instills a type of calm and peace felt deep within, which then in turn creates happiness.

Gratitude in Action: Say "thank you" to everyone you meet who helps you today.

87.

---·❀·---

❝It is in your hands to create a better world for all who live in it.❞

~ Nelson Mandela

---·❀·---

A child's mind is filled with wonder and excitement. It is open to new ideas and is willing to try anything and everything. As adults in this world, it's our job to guide these young minds as they grow and explore, without squashing their creativity. The same can be said for ourselves—each one of us has a child inside looking for guidance and encouragement to create and live in a better world.

Gratitude in Action: Spend some time today encouraging a child with positive words and actions.

88.

❝Be a warrior not a worrier.❞

~ Unknown

Your happiness is solely dependent upon you. But when you encounter a really tough situation, it may be easy to slide down the path of worry. If you find that you do, come to a halt and think again. Consider what could go right in the situation, and what you could do to make the outcome better.

Gratitude in Action: Call to mind the very thing you are having difficulty accomplishing. Determine three steps you can take toward a solution. Pick one step to work on today, plan to do another step tomorrow, and the last step the day after that.

89.

" Every day we are faced with great opportunities disguised as difficult circumstances. "

~ Dr. Samantha Madhosingh

If you live your life dwelling on what can go wrong, things will continue to go in that direction. Instead look at each negative circumstance as an opportunity to show the world what you have—the inner strength that is waiting for an opportunity to make itself known. Every day is an opportunity to shine in the face of challenges.

Gratitude in Action: Banish the words "I can't," "I am a failure," and "I'll try" from your vocabulary (both out loud and in your head) for the entire day. Focus only on what you CAN and WILL do.

90.

❦

"Amongst all other vices there is none I hate more than cruelty, both by nature and judgment, as the extremist of all vices."

~ Montaigne

❦

None of us want to hurt people, but sometimes it happens. A comment slips out before thinking or we join others in sharing gossip. Be careful in living in this realm for long, as a judgmental attitude can be contagious. It can grow until we are not only critical of others, but of ourselves.

Gratitude in Action: Catch yourself being judgmental or critical of yourself or others…and just STOP. Reframe how you are thinking and change your perspective.

91.

❝We gain strength by sharing strength.❞

~ Don Ward

We impact people's lives each and every day, both positively and negatively, with the interactions we have with them. Oftentimes, you may not be aware of the impact you have on others. Think about it for yourself though: Who is the person who has most influenced and guided you? Perhaps it was your father or mother, a teacher or mentor, or even a friend. Have you ever thought about letting that person know how much you appreciate them and the words they shared in giving you encouragement? It would be a gift to share with them the influence they have had on you and your life.

Gratitude in Action: Write a letter to someone who has made a difference in your life.

92.

❝Kindness in words creates confidence.
Kindness in thinking creates profoundness.
Kindness in giving creates love.❞

~ Lao Tzu

It has been said that when you help someone you help yourself.
When you teach, you learn. When you give, you receive. Sharing
yourself with your child, neighbor, or as a volunteer to someone
you don't know, creates a joy unto itself. Providing assistance to
another human, or perhaps an animal, reaps rewards unlike
anything else. It happens in the name of kindness.

Gratitude in Action: Offer to do something for someone that
you know they don't enjoy doing or are unable to do, such as
organizing their closet, walking their dog, raking the leaves, or
mowing their lawn. Make this offer freely with no expectation of
something returned.

93.

❝Isn't it kind of silly to think that tearing someone else down builds you up?❞

~ Sean Covey

Maybe you have been the brunt of someone talking negatively behind your back. Or you join in when others are talking about someone who is not present. It can be easy to talk about or be critical or judgmental of someone who's not there, but what is it saying about you? Whether you join in on the conversation or do nothing, damage is being created to not only the person who is being discussed but to you as well. Turn the table around, put yourself into the other's shoes, and begin to spread joy and positivity.

Gratitude in Action: Be committed to no gossip today. When you speak of others, find something positive to say about them.

94.

❝Giving encouragement to others is a most welcome gift, for the results of it are lifted spirits, increased self-worth, and a hopeful future.❞

~ Florence Littauer

Ever have one of those days where everything was going well? You revel in one thing after another falling into place and making you smile. One of the best ways to celebrate that sense of joy is to share it with another. Encouraging someone who might be feeling down is just what the doctor ordered to keep your spirits soaring high—and helping another along the way.

Gratitude in Action: Say something encouraging and supportive to someone who needs it.

95.

❝Gratitude is not only the greatest of virtues, but the parent of all others.❞

~ Cicero

Being thankful is the key to feeling better yourself. Expressing gratitude creates a surge of positive feelings throughout your body and makes others feel great, too. When you practice gratitude, you also are more likely to keep life's big picture in mind and stay calm in situations that used to cause anxiety. The best thing is that you can make these positive differences in small and simple ways.

Gratitude in Action: Write a handwritten note of thanks to your server at a restaurant...or to someone you meet today who, because of his or her very presence, brightens your day.

96.

❝Never pass up an opportunity to speak a kind word of appreciation. There are six billion people on the planet, and 5.9 billion of them go to bed every night starving for one honest word of appreciation.❞

~ Matthew Kelly

There are many people who go through the day hearing no words of praise or thanks from another. It's not that they don't engage with others, it's just that the utterance of "thank you" doesn't come. It's a missed opportunity to make a positive change in the world. Being generous with your thanks and gratitude can make a big difference to someone who is starving for appreciation.

Gratitude in Action: Send an email of appreciation to someone who may not know how much you appreciate them—and let them know you just wanted to express your gratitude, so they don't need to write back

97.

---❀---

❝People who are the happiest don't necessarily have everything, but they are thankful for everything they do have.**❞**

~ Dr. Samantha Madhosingh

---❀---

Whether you call it venting, complaining or whining, partaking in negative talk can impact your wellbeing. It stops the flow of abundance and puts a glaring spotlight on what you want less of in life. To feel more content and happy, make an effort to count your blessings. Identify what's going right and dwell on that. As your gratitude expands, you'll find that more things you like and appreciate will come into your life.

Gratitude in Action: Make a commitment today to avoid complaining. Banish words of complaint.

98.

~ Rattana Hetzel

What if all the love in the world stemmed from inside you? It can start as a seed in your heart and then branch out through your thoughts, actions and words so others may feel love, too. You are made stronger by practicing self-love, and that love radiates to the people around you. Connect with yourself and love yourself. It all starts with you.

Gratitude in Action: Write yourself a love letter. Describe all the things you admire about yourself.

99.

❝Feeling gratitude and not expressing it is like wrapping a present and not giving it.❞

~ William Arthur Ward

When you look for ways to express gratitude, you'll see many opportunities. The key is to take advantage of those occasions to say "thanks" and "I appreciate you" to others. Although it may feel awkward at first, once you get in the practice you'll become more comfortable with it. You'll reap the benefits of expressing thanks for the people, activities and items that are in your life, and it is satisfying to see how others blossom when you show your gratitude.

Gratitude in Action: Have family dinners regularly and discuss what each person present is thankful for. Be sure to also express appreciation for each other and look for ways to make showing gratitude a daily practice in your relationships.

100.

❝Passion doesn't come from business or books or even a connection with another person. It is a connection to your own life force, the world around you and the spirit that connects us all. You are the source. Books, work, music, people, sunsets all provide sparks, but only you can light the fire.**❞**

~ Jennifer James

Life is more than making a to-do list and marking off items as they are completed. That's not why we were put on this earth. Instead, you are given a sense of curiosity about all kinds of interesting things, along with the ability to create art, music and thoughts of your own. Take advantage of the opportunities around you and enjoy something bigger than can be captured on a to-do list.

Gratitude in Action: Plan to spend the day enjoying a passion you're sometimes too busy to fit in.

Notes

Notes

Notes

Notes

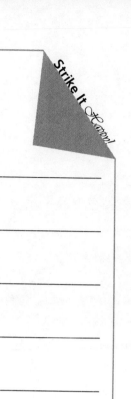